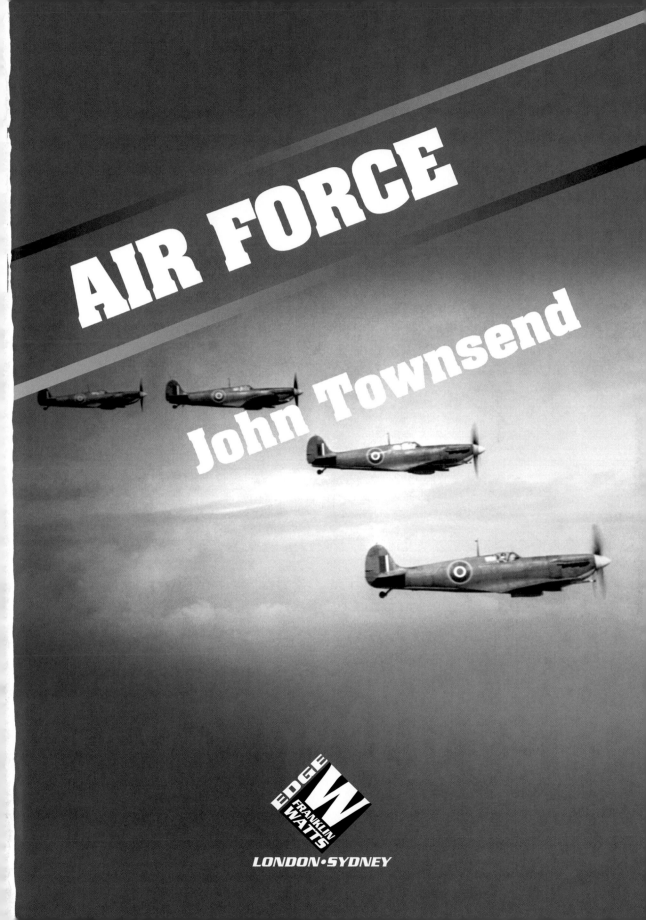

# AIR FORCE

## John Townsend

EDGE
**W**
FRANKLIN
WATTS

*LONDON · SYDNEY*

First published in 2013 by
Franklin Watts
338 Euston Road
London NW1 3BH

Franklin Watts Australia
Level 17/207 Kent Street
Sydney NSW 2000

Series editor: Adrian Cole, John C. Miles
Art direction: Peter Scoulding
Design: Simon Borrough
Picture research: Diana Morris

A CIP catalogue record for this book is available from the British Library.

Dewey number: 940.5

(HB) ISBN: 978 1 4451 2326 4
(Library eBook) ISBN: 978 1 4451 2571 8

Printed in China

Franklin Watts is a division of Hachette Children's Books,
an Hachette UK company.

www.hachette.co.uk

Picture credits:
Cody Images: 6l, 8, 9b, 13, 19, 21t, 25, 27, 28.
Flight Collection/Topfoto: 23b.
The Granger Collection/Topfoto: 14t.
Hulton Archive/Getty Images: front cover.
Khomenko/RIA Novosti/Topfoto: 16.
The National Archives/HIP/Topfoto: 4t, 5, 9t, 15b.
Picturepoint/Topham: 1, 4c, 6r, 10, 12, 23t, 29.
RIA Novosti/Topfoto: 17tr.
Roger-Viollet/Topfoto: 18.
Topfoto: 17, 21b, 24.
ullsteinbild /Topfoto: 7, 22t, 22b.
US Navy: 20.
Anatoly Sergeev-Vasiliev/RIA Novosti/Topfoto: 17tl.
Wikipedia: 19cr.

*Every attempt has been made to clear copyright. Should there be any
inadvertent omission please apply to the publisher for rectification.*

# Contents

War in the Air                                        4

Hitler's air force – the *Luftwaffe*   6

The Royal Air Force                             8

Fighter Aircraft                                   10

Bombers                                            12

Case Study –                                       14
The Battle of Britain

Soviet Air Force                                  16

Japanese Air Force                            18

US Air Force                                         20

Jet Power                                            22

Night Raids                                         24

Case Study –                                       26
The Battle of the Philippine Sea

Final Air Assaults                             28

World War II Timeline                     30

Glossary                                             31

Index                                                  32

# War in the Air

World War II (1939—1945) was the first war to send hundreds of thousands of advanced aircraft into combat. With such air power, the war was like no other, as planes attacked anywhere behind enemy lines, including civilian as well as military targets. This was very much everyone's war.

**BACK THEM UP!**

 *All air forces in World War II held recruitment drives.*

# ACTION STATS

### Aircraft Available In Europe in WWII

| Date | British | US | Soviet | Total Allied | German |
|------|---------|------|--------|--------------|--------|
| June 1942 | 9,500 | — | 2,100 | 11,600 | 3,700 |
| December 1942 | 11,300 | 1,300 | 3,800 | 16,400 | 3,400 |
| June 1943 | 12,700 | 5,000 | 5,600 | 23,300 | 4,600 |
| December 1943 | 11,800 | 7,500 | 8,800 | 28,100 | 4,700 |
| June 1944 | 13,200 | 11,800 | 14,700 | 39,700 | 4,600 |
| December 1944 | 14,500 | 12,200 | 15,800 | 42,500 | 8,500 |

Aircraft were important for attack, defence and reconnaissance (information gathering). Studying aerial photographs helped the planning of many ground operations.

*Surrender! The crew of a damaged German submarine gives up after an attack by an aircraft of Britain's Royal Air Force.*

Aerial bombardment disrupted or destroyed industry, airfields, troops, ships, defences, railways, communications, roads and bridges. The bombing of towns and cities caused massive civilian casualties. This was aimed at weakening public morale, as well as the will of political leaders.

The battle for air supremacy in World War II came at a great cost in human lives.

# AF FACTS

**Allies: air forces fighting against the Axis powers (France, Britain and its Empire, the USA and Russia)**
**Axis: air forces opposing the Allies (Germany, Japan, Italy and a few other countries)**

# Hitler's air force
# – the *Luftwaffe*

In 1934, Adolf Hitler became the leader of Germany. He and his Nazi Party rapidly began building up the country's military strength, including its air force.

By 1935, the *Luftwaffe* (German air force) was established, and thousands of new aircraft were built. Commanded by World War I pilot Hermann Goering, the Luftwaffe became the largest and most powerful air force in Europe by the start of World War II in 1939.

*Nazi leader Adolf Hitler (left) and Luftwaffe chief Hermann Goering (right).*

Germany began World War II by invading Poland in September 1939, with the Luftwaffe backing up the *Wehrmacht* (German ground forces) with 1,200 fighter aircraft and 1,750 bombers. The main German aircraft were:

**Messerschmitt Bf109**: a key modern fighter plane with mounted machine guns and/or cannons;

**Junkers Ju87 Stuka**: a two-man (pilot and gunner) dive bomber and ground attack aircraft;

**Dornier Do17**: a 'light bomber' with crew of four: the pilot, a bomb-aimer and two gunners;

**Heinkel He111**: a fast 'medium bomber' with a crew of five.

*A formidable weapon — Heinkel He111s flying in formation.*

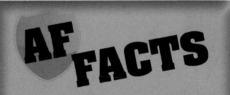

# The Royal Air Force

The massive Nazi aircraft-building programme of the 1930s meant that Britain's Royal Air Force lagged behind. When war broke out in 1939, the RAF was catching up, but it suffered heavy losses at the beginning of the war as it fought against more advanced German aircraft.

*Restored World War II Spitfires fly over England.*

As Germany invaded other European countries such as Belgium and France, RAF bombers attacked the advancing German army — but were often outgunned and outmanoeuvred. British and French armies were forced to retreat, with almost 200,000 British soldiers and 140,000 French being rescued by boats from Dunkirk while under attack from the Luftwaffe. The RAF fought back but with serious losses; 177 of its aircraft were shot down, including 106 fighters (Hurricanes and Spitfires).

Facing heavy losses, the RAF had to ask the USA for extra pilots and planes. The first year of World War II was the darkest of times for the RAF.

*This World War II poster attempted to boost morale by boasting of the RAF's strength.*

*RAF pilots relax in between missions at an airfield. A Hurricane fighter sits ready to fly behind them.*

# Fighter Aircraft

Unlike bombers and attack aircraft that strike ground targets, fighter aircraft are designed for air-to-air combat with enemy planes. They are built for speed and manoeuvrability.

At the start of World War II, the Luftwaffe's feared Messerschmitt Bf109 was the key fighter in air battles over France. It was designed in the 1930s, and was the first of the modern fighters with a closed canopy, a powerful liquid-cooled engine and retractable landing gear.

The Bf109 could reach a maximum speed of 640 kph and had a range of 850 km before needing to refuel.

The legendary Spitfire of the RAF had a shorter range (760 km) than the Bf109 but it could climb higher than its rival in combat.

*Having shot down a German Dornier Do17 bomber (left), an RAF Hurricane sweeps away to look for a new target.*

German Bf109s lined up at an airfield.

A dogfight was the term for aerial combat between fighter aircraft. Many dogfights took place over the English Channel at the start of the war. Fighter pilots needed great skill to manoeuvre at close range, trying to dodge bullets while aiming gunfire at the enemy.

Some fighter aircraft were designed to escort bomber aircraft to and from their targets. They had to be able to fly long distances without refuelling and be able to fight off enemy attacks on the bomber formations.

The American P-51 Mustang was often used as an escort fighter in World War II. Armed with machine guns, bombs or rockets, it carried a huge fuel load and was one of the best all-round fighters of the war.

# ACTION STATS

The Messerschmitt Bf109 was mass-produced from 1936 to the end of the war. Almost 34,000 were built, making it the most produced Axis aircraft. They were armed with 9 mm machine guns and 20 mm cannons in the wings.

# Bombers

Throughout World War II, air forces were constantly developing bigger and better aircraft to carry bigger bomb loads. Bombers were of three basic types.

**Light Bombers** These planes carried a bomb load of 500–1,000 kg. They were used for short bombing missions and also for reconnaissance work. The United States supplied the RAF with the Lockheed Hudson and Martin Baltimore aircraft as light bombers.

De Havilland Mosquitos of the RAF at an airbase.

**Medium Bombers** These could carry larger bomb loads (45,000–100,000 kg) for longer distances than light bombers. The United States built over 7,000 Douglas A-20 Havoc medium bombers during the war — these were used by many Allied air forces.

The De Havilland Mosquito was a British medium bomber used from 1942 in high-speed missions attacking factories and other targets in Germany and occupied Europe.

## AF FACTS

Dive bombers, such as Germany's Junkers Ju87 Stuka would dive in a swarm from 4,500 m to a release altitude of 900 m in about 30 seconds. Their high level of accuracy made these aircraft much feared in air raids.

An Avro Lancaster
drops its full bomb load.

**12,000 heavy bombers were shot down in World War II. Between 1939 and 1945 the Allies dropped 3.4 million tons of bombs (2.8 million tons on Germany).**

**Heavy Bombers** These four-engined aircraft were used chiefly by the USA and Britain. The USA's B-17 Flying Fortress was the world's first 4-engine long-range heavy bomber. The RAF's Avro Lancaster became famous for its use in the so-called 'Dambuster' raids of 1943. Heavy bombers like these were used to smash the industrial centres of Axis countries.

# Case Study – The Battle of Britain

In the summer of 1940, Hitler planned to invade Britain. The Luftwaffe increased aerial bombing raids on British cities in the 'Blitz', but also set out to destroy the RAF in aerial combat.

## ACTION STATS

The Blitz lasted from 7 September 1940 to 21 May 1941. British cities targeted by the Luftwaffe included London, Birmingham, Liverpool, Plymouth and Glasgow. Over 40,000 people in Britain were killed in air raids, but in the end the Blitz was a failure — Britain didn't surrender!

# AF FACTS

**Battle of Britain**
**Date: July – Oct 1940**
**Place: The skies above southern England**
**Code Name: Operation Sealion (the name given by Hitler for Nazi Germany's planned invasion of Great Britain)**

Spitfires of the RAF engage German bombers heading for British cities in the Battle of Britain.

"Never in the field of human conflict was so much owed by so many to so few."

WINSTON CHURCHILL

This poster uses British Prime Minister Winston Churchill's famous words to celebrate the courage of RAF pilots.

Throughout August and September, the Luftwaffe's attacks continued. Despite being outnumbered, the RAF fought back with increasing success. There were heavy losses on both sides. The Luftwaffe then concentrated on bombing cities rather than aerial combat. This gave the RAF's exhausted crews time to recover.

By October, the Luftwaffe was losing the battle because its fighters had only limited time for flying over Britain before they ran out of fuel and ammunition. Germany lost the Battle of Britain — the first major Axis defeat of World War II — and called off the invasion.

# Soviet Air Force

One of the reasons that Germany lost the Battle of Britain was because Nazi leaders were concentrating their efforts elsewhere. They were focusing on the east and planning Operation Barbarossa: the invasion of Russia.

Russia's air force (the VVS) was quickly training pilots and ground support crews but they still weren't ready when Germany attacked Russia in 1941. Despite suffering many losses, the Soviet 'Red Air Force' had three powerful aircraft:

## ACTION STATS

In the first few days of Operation Barbarossa in June 1941, the Luftwaffe destroyed 2,000 Soviet aircraft, most of them on the ground — with only 35 Luftwaffe aircraft lost.

• **The Ilyushin Il-2** was a fast two-man dive-bomber with armour to withstand direct hits. It was known as the 'Flying Tank', and the Soviets built 36,000 of them during the war. Its two cannons and two machine guns, as well as a 660-kg bomb load, made this a powerful plane for supporting Russian ground troops.

*Left and above (side and top/bottom views), the versatile Ilyushin Il-2.*

• **The Petlyakov PE-8** bomber had a long range so it could reach targets inside Germany.

• **The Yakovlev Yak-1** single-engine fighter was effective in attacking the Luftwaffe at close range.

*The Yak-1 was manoeuvrable, fast and well armed.*

# AF FACTS

**One thousand Russian women volunteered to become pilots. Three entire regiments of the air force were made up solely of women, who regularly flew on bombing raids. The most famous was Lilya Litvyak (pictured), known as the 'White Rose of Stalingrad'. She shot down 22 enemy aircraft before she was shot down herself.**

# Japanese Air Force

While the war in Europe spread, Japan was building its air power so it could take over areas around the Pacific Ocean. By 1941 the Japanese Army Air Force had about 1,500 aircraft ready to attack land targets, while the Japanese Navy Air Force had more than 1,400 planes.

Fearing the United States would try to stop its plans for Pacific domination, on 7 December 1941 Japan sent a huge force of aircraft to attack the US Fleet at Pearl Harbor in Hawaii.

In just two hours 18 US warships, 188 aircraft and 2,403 servicemen were lost in the attack. Both the USA and Japan had now entered World War II.

Japan's air force had many successes. but the growing strength of the US Air Force led to Japan losing air supremacy. In late 1944 the Japanese used a surprising new tactic — the kamikaze suicide plane. Japanese pilots began crashing their aircraft into US ships. Many kamikaze pilots were only 18 to 24 years old. Most believed killing themselves for Japan was a very honourable thing to do.

*A young Japanese kamikaze pilot poses for his last photograph.*

An attacking kamikaze aircraft heads straight for a US ship in the Pacific.

The Japanese Mitsubishi A-6 'Zero' fighter was an outstanding aircraft.

## AF FACTS

The first Japanese kamikaze attack was in October 1944. A Japanese plane flew straight into an Australian navy ship, killing 30 sailors.

## ACTION STATS

By the end of the war over 2,500 Japanese pilots had killed themselves on kamikaze missions. About 5,000 US and Allied sailors died in kamikaze attacks.

# US Air Force

As soon as the US joined the war, it launched air attacks against Japanese bases in the Pacific. The first air raid by the United States to strike at Japan itself was in April 1942, when sixteen B-25 bombers took off from the aircraft carrier USS *Hornet*.

*Bound for Tokyo, a B-25 bomber takes off from the deck of USS* Hornet.

Their bombs caused little damage and the planes, which had no way of returning, were lost. Three crew members died and eight were captured. Despite this, the raid shocked the Japanese people and leaders, who had thought they were beyond the range of US bombers. It also boosted US morale after the disaster at Pearl Harbor in 1941.

 *Wildcats were also used by Britain's Royal Navy. They are shown here on the deck of the carrier HMS* Formidable.

*Hellcats on a mission.*

A US Navy aircraft carrier could hold nearly twice the aircraft of a similar-sized Japanese carrier. The Grumman F4F Wildcat was very short and had folding wings — perfect for storing on the decks of aircraft carriers. Its successor, the F6F Hellcat, could outfight Japanese Zero fighters as it was faster and sturdier. A short burst from its six machine guns was usually enough to bring down a Zero.

# Jet Power

World War II saw the development of the first jet aircraft. Powering planes with jet engines provided far greater speed for swifter attacks.

*Messerschmitt Me262 in camouflage paint. One German pilot said flying it was 'as though angels were pushing'.*

Both Britain and Germany were developing jet engines at the start of the war. However, it was the German Messerschmitt Me262 that became the world's first operational jet-powered fighter. In the last year of the war it shot down many allied aircraft. Germany also built the Heinkel He162 fighter (below), but metal was so scarce that the plane had to be made mainly of wood.

## ACTION STATS

The Luftwaffe built 170 wooden Heinkel He162 jets. They could reach a speed of 900 kph — but could only fly for 30 minutes before refuelling.

The V-1 'doodlebug' had a single engine mounted at the rear of the craft.

The German V-1 flying bomb had a jet engine but it was unmanned — like a modern cruise missile. It was developed by the Luftwaffe towards the end of the war. With a speed of 640 kph and a range of 250 km, many of these 'doodlebugs' were fired at London and Antwerp.

In 1942, America's first jet fighter, the Bell XP-59 — was tested. The US Air Force was not impressed by its performance so production stopped and it never went into combat.

However, the Allies did fight with Britain's first jet fighter — with turbojet engines developed by Sir Frank Whittle. The Gloster Meteor first flew on missions in July 1944 with the RAF's 616 Squadron. The squadron's first mission was to attack V-1 flying bombs. By January 1945 Meteors were stationed in Belgium, supporting Allied ground forces as they fought their way to Berlin.

The Gloster Meteor was Britain's first jet fighter. Its top speed was more than 900 kph.

# Night Raids

Many air force missions took place at night.
Aircraft were obviously safer if they couldn't
be seen by the enemy below but there
were risks in flying in the dark. Aircraft in
World War II didn't have satellite navigation
systems, so finding targets and not getting
lost were real problems.

No night-fighter aircraft existed at the start of
World War II and pilots feared searchlights and anti-aircraft
guns. Air forces developed night fighters designed especially for
air combat in the dark. Radar was one of the important systems
for guiding pilots in low visibility.

*Lancaster bombers
of the RAF on a night
mission to bomb
Germany.*

The Northrop P-61 Black Widow was the first US military aircraft designed especially for night attacks on enemy aircraft, using radar. The first test flight was in May 1942 and its first missions were in 1944.

The P-61 Black Widow had a distinctive twin-boom tail design.

## ACTION STATS

### Lancaster Bomber

| | |
|---|---|
| Length: | 21.11 m |
| Wingspan: | 31.09 m |
| Bomb load: | 6,300 kg (normal load) |
| Firepower: | 8 x .303-cal Browning machine guns |
| Range: | Up to 4,073 km |
| Power: | 4 x RR Merlin |
| Crew: | 7 |

RAF Bomber Command sent many night raids over Germany — using Lancaster bombers to target the Luftwaffe's aircraft factories. By July 1943, German night fighters were having a success rate of 5 per cent for shooting down RAF bombers. Night fighters used radar to find them in the dark. To jam enemy radar, bombers dropped thousands of aluminium strips called 'chaff'. These clouds of metal pieces not only confused the radar systems of night fighters but they also puzzled people living below when it rained aluminium!

# Case Study – The Battle of the Philippine Sea

Landing aircraft at night on moving carriers in the middle of the ocean could be treacherous. It proved to be deadly for American pilots not trained to land in the dark, when returning from a major air battle in the Pacific in 1944.

The battle was the last of five between Japanese and American aircraft carriers at the Mariana Islands. It was also a major defeat for Japanese forces.

During the battle 77 US dive-bombers, 54 torpedo planes and 85 fighters took off from American carriers in Task Force 58 to attack the Japanese fleet. Hundreds of Japanese planes from nearby bases flew in to the battle but over 350 of them were shot down on the first day.

## AF FACTS

**The Battle of the Philippine Sea**
**Date:** 19-20 June, 1944
**Place:** The Mariana Islands (north-west Pacific Ocean between Japan & New Guinea)
**Nickname:** 'Great Marianas Turkey Shoot'

# ACTION STATS

**Casualties and losses in the Battle of the Philippine Sea**

## US
1 battleship damaged
123 aircraft destroyed

## Japan
3 fleet carriers sunk
2 fuel ships sunk
550–645 aircraft
   destroyed
6 other ships damaged

The first US aircraft began to return to Task Force 58 as night fell but they couldn't find the carriers in the dark. They were also running out of fuel. Despite the danger of being seen by enemy aircraft or submarines, the US carriers shone searchlights into the sky to show their position. Destroyers fired shells to help the aircraft find the task force but 80 of the returning planes were lost. Of the 209 aircrew,160 were eventually rescued from the sea.

*US servicemen watch the aerial action in the Battle of the Philippine Sea.*

# Final Air Assaults

On D-Day (6 June 1944), Allied troops landed on French beaches to begin freeing Europe from the Nazis. Allied air forces engaged in major attacks to weaken further the Luftwaffe's airpower.

Eventually the Allies advanced to Berlin, where air raids continued to weaken Nazi morale. The Luftwaffe was outnumbered, out of fuel and defeated. The war in Europe was finally over in May 1945.

The war with Japan continued for another three months until the US bombed its cities like never before. When Japanese leaders refused to surrender, the US sent a Boeing B-29 Super Fortress bomber with an atomic bomb on board.

 *Colonel Paul Tibbets in the cockpit of Enola Gay, the aircraft that dropped the first atomic bomb on 6 August 1945.*

It dropped the first ever bomb of its kind on the Japanese city of Hiroshima — causing huge destruction. Three days later Japan's leaders had not surrendered, so the US dropped another atom bomb — this time on the city of Nagasaki.

Japan eventually surrendered and the Allies celebrated VJ (Victory in Japan) Day on 15 August 1945 — although the surrender wasn't signed until 2 September. World War II was finally over — after six devastating years and the most intensive air campaigns in history.

## AF FACTS

VJ Day marked not only the end of the war in the Pacific, but also the end of World War II. In Britain, huge crowds gathered to cheer King George VI and Prime Minister Winston Churchill — while the RAF provided the triumphant flypast!

*An exhausted US airman celebrates VE (Victory in Europe) day beside his aircraft on 8 May 1945.*

NAZIS QUIT! Dönitz Gives Ord...

# World War II Timeline

- **1939: 1 September** – Germany invades Poland; Great Britain and France declare war against Germany.

- **1940:** the Luftwaffe engages the RAF in the Battle of Britain then attacks British cities in the Blitz.

- **1941: 7 December** – Japan bombs Pearl Harbor, bringing the USA into the war.

- **1942: April** – 272 British bombers of the RAF attack Hamburg at night – the largest raid yet on a single target.

- **1942: July** – the first US B-17 'Flying Fortress' arrives in the UK.

- **1943: January** – the RAF attacks Berlin for the first time with Mosquito aircraft.

- **1943: 14 October, 'Black Thursday'** – nearly 600 crew members are lost in an Allied bombing raid on a factory in Germany.

- **1944: March** – the Allies bomb Berlin, dropping thousands of tons of bombs, with heavy losses on both sides.

- **1944: 6 June** – after a night-time air assault, over 160,000 Allied troops land along the Normandy coast on 'D-Day'.

- **1944: 19-20 June** – the Battle of the Philippine Sea – US fighter planes help to defeat the Japanese fleet.

- **1945: 10 April** – Allied aircraft shoot down half of the German Messerschmitt Me262 jet fighter planes. The loss is fatal to the Luftwaffe and their defence of Berlin is abandoned.

- **1945: 30 April** – Adolf Hitler commits suicide in his bunker, and within days Germany surrenders.

- **1945: 6, 9 August** – the US drops atomic bombs on Japan.

- **1945: 15 August** – Japan surrenders, officially ending World War II.

# Glossary

**aerial** – operating from aircraft in the sky

**altitude** – the height of an aircraft above the ground

**blitz** – a sustained series of air raids

**civilians** – ordinary members of the public who do not belong to the armed forces

**closed canopy** – the sliding cover that shields a pilot inside an aircraft's cockpit

**dogfight** – a battle at close range between fighter planes

**kamikaze** – in World War II, a Japanese aircraft loaded with explosives making a suicidal crash on an enemy target

**Luftwaffe** – the German air force before and during World War II

**manoeuvrability** – the ability to turn, climb and dive quickly while in flight

**morale** – the mood and state of mind of a person or group

**RADAR** – stands for radio detecting and ranging – using radio waves for locating objects

**reconnaissance** – a mission to gain information about the enemy

**retractable** – able to be pulled in. Retractable landing gear/wheels retract into the wings and/or fuselage of a plane to reduce drag and improve air speed

**squadron** – a working unit in an air force consisting of aircraft, the pilots to fly them and the ground crew to look after them

**turbojet** – a jet engine using a turbine to compress an air-fuel mixture in a combustion chamber. A spark ignites the mixture and this creates a jet of hot gas, which pushes the aircraft forwards

# Index

**air raids** 5, 12, 13, 14, 15, 20, 24, 25
**atomic bombs** 28, 29

**B-17 Flying Fortress** 13
**B-25 bomber** 20
**Battle of Britain** 14–15, 16
**Battle of the Philippine Sea** 26–27
**Blitz** 14
**Boeing B-29 Super Fortress** 28

**D-Day** 28
**De Havilland Mosquito** 12
**dogfights** 11
**Dornier Do17** 7, 11
**Douglas A-20 Havoc** 12
**Dunkirk** 9

**Gloster Meteor** 23
**Goering, Hermann** 6
**Grumman F4F Wildcat** 21
**Grumman F6F Hellcat** 21

**Hawker Hurricane** 8, 9, 11
**Heinkel He111** 7
**Heinkel He162** 22
**Hitler, Adolf** 6, 14, 15
**HMS *Formidable*** 21

**Ilyushin Il-2** 16

**Japanese Air Force** 5, 18–19, 26–27
**Junkers Ju87 Stuka** 7, 12

**kamikaze attacks** 18, 19

**Lancaster bombers** 13, 24, 25
**Litvyak, Lilya** 17
**Lockheed Hudson** 12
**Luftwaffe** 5, 6–17, 22, 23, 25, 28

**Martin Baltimore** 12
**Messerschmitt Bf109** 7, 10 11, 22
**Messerschmitt Me262** 22
**Mitsubishi A-6 'Zero'** 18, 21

**night fighters** 24–25
**Northrop P-61 Black Widow** 25

**P-51 Mustang** 11
**Pearl Harbor** 18, 21
**Petlyakov PE-8** 17

**radar** 24, 25
**reconnaissance** 4, 12
**Royal Air Force** 5, 8–15, 21, 23, 24, 25, 29

**Soviet air force** 5, 16–17
**Supermarine Spitfire** 8, 9, 10, 15

**US Air Force** 5, 11, 13, 19, 20–21, 23, 25, 26–27, 28, 29
**USS *Hornet*** 20

**V-1 doodlebug** 23

**Yakovlev Yak-1** 17